Teach Me
SPORTS
HOCKEY

BY BARRY DREAYER

Updated Edition

General Publishing Group, Inc.
Los Angeles

Publisher: W. Quay Hays
Editor: Barry Dreayer
Managing Editor: Colby Allerton
Cover Design: Kurt Wahlner
Production Director: Nadeen Torio
Production Assistant: Catherine Vo Bailey
Copy Editor: Peter Hoffman

Special thanks to the following individuals for their
assistance with The Hockey Edition: Curt Bennett,
Vicki Blumenfeld, Joe Bucchino, Al Dreayer, Paul Joffe,
Mel Powell, Barbara Webb, Rick Webb, Sierra Webb,
Doug Wilson.

The *Teach Me Sports*™ series is published by
General Publishing Group, Inc.,
2701 Ocean Park Blvd., Suite 140,
Santa Monica, CA 90405
310-314-4000.

Library of Congress Catalog Card Number
95-75162

ISBN 1-881649-35-0

10 9 8 7 6 5 4 3 2

Printed in the USA by RR Donnelley & Sons Company

INTRODUCTION

To many fans, hockey is the most exciting sport to watch. The action is constant, the contact between opposing players is entertaining and the speed of the players' skating is thrilling. However, the different types of violations and penalties make it frustrating for those who do not closely follow the game. *Teach Me Sports Hockey* explains and illustrates these violations and penalties along with the strategy, terminology, scoring and statistics that are a part of hockey.

This book begins with the assumption that the reader is aware that hockey involves "players skating on ice, using sticks to hit a hard rubber disk into the opponent's goal." From this basic premise, the book presents a crash course on becoming an educated hockey fan. It is meant to be used while watching the games on TV and/or in person.

Teach Me Sports Hockey is based on the professional game played by the National Hockey League (NHL).

The book does not attempt to cover every one of hockey's hundreds of rules and situations, and many examples have been simplified for the sake of clarity. The text shows the WHY behind the WHAT. (For example: Why a goalie may leave the ice late in the game.)

So, come on and join the fun by learning the game!

Teach Me SPORTS
JOIN THE FUN BY LEARNING THE GAME

THE HOCKEY EDITION

THE ORIGIN OF HOCKEY

No true evidence exists as to when and how hockey started. Hockey's roots are from field hockey and other games such as bandy and shinny that involved using a stick to hit a ball between two poles. Many claim that in 1855, British soldiers in Canada were the first to play hockey on ice.

In 1879, rules were standardized and a flat, disk-shaped puck was used instead of a ball. There were thirty players on each team (soon reduced to nine) and the first team to score three goals won the game. Substitutions were not allowed. If a player could no longer play because of an injury, the opposing team had to remove a player to make the teams equal.

Referees used to have to place the puck between opposing players' sticks during face-offs. Broken knuckles were not uncommon for these brave officials. Fortunately for them, they were allowed to drop the puck between opposing players' sticks beginning in 1914.

Goalies had to stand in one spot. They could not even drop to their knees to block a shot. If they did, an automatic fine of two dollars would be assessed. If a goalie dropped to his knees to block a second shot during a game, he would be fined three dollars and given a five-minute penalty. That changed in 1917, the first year of the National Hockey League.

Hockey continued to evolve into the modern-day version enjoyed by millions.

GOAL

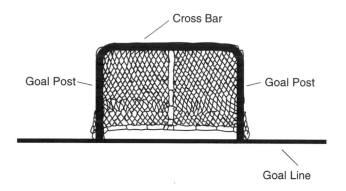

BASIC RULES AND OBJECTIVES

The primary objective is to score more goals than the opposing team.

- A GOAL is scored when a player's STICK causes the PUCK (hockey's "ball") to cross entirely over the opponent's GOAL LINE between the GOAL POSTS and underneath the CROSS BAR.

Each team is allowed no more than 6 players on the ice (called the RINK) at one time.

- The team that has possession of the puck is on OFFENSE and is the ATTACKING TEAM.
- The team without possession of the puck is on DEFENSE and is the DEFENDING TEAM.

The puck is a hard rubber disk that is 3 inches in diameter and 1 inch thick.

- Pucks are kept frozen because cold pucks move more easily on the ice. If the pucks were not frozen, they would have a tendency to bounce along the ice.

There are 60 minutes of play that are divided into three 20-minute PERIODS. An intermission takes place between each period. During both intermissions, the ice is usually FLOODED (refreshed by spraying, skimming and chilling) using a machine called a ZAMBONI.

- In the regular season, if teams are tied after 60 minutes, they play up to five more minutes, called SUDDEN DEATH OVERTIME.
    - The first team to score in the overtime wins.
    - If teams are still tied after five minutes, the game ends as a tie.
- During the PLAYOFFS, a tie is not acceptable because a winner must be determined. Therefore, if teams are tied after 60 minutes, they play 20-minute sudden death overtime periods until a team scores to win the game.

- Time stops during a game when play is halted after:

Former Boston Bruin center Derek Sanderson favored the following strategy during face-offs: "One of the key elements to winning a face-off is cheating. You've got to cheat because it's too difficult to win most of them fair and square."

- A team scores.
- A violation is committed (discussed in detail later).
- The puck is unplayable such as when it leaves the playing area.
- The primary official (the REFEREE) cannot see the puck.
    1. Broadcasters may say, "Play is stopped because the referee lost sight of the puck."
- TEAM TIME OUT — When time has already stopped, a team may request a thirty-second delay before restarting the action.
    a. Each team is allowed one time out in a game.
    b. A team requests a time out to discuss strategy or halt the opposing team's momentum.

If a player is replaced by a substitute, he is allowed to return to the game.

- Hockey is the only sport that allows substitutions to take place during the action of the game (called CHANGING ON THE FLY)—a stop in play is not required.
    - What is required is that the player being replaced must be within 5 feet of his PLAYERS' BENCH (not precisely enforced by the officials) before his substitute may come on the ice, and
    - The puck must be away from his players' bench. Imagine the chaos if substitutes were allowed to enter the ice near the place where players on both teams were gathered going after the puck.
- Substitutions are usually done in groups—the three FORWARDS or the two DEFENSEMEN (discussed in detail later).

The game begins with a FACE-OFF (sometimes called a DRAW, like in old western television shows and movies) at the center of the rink.

Most first-year players (called ROOKIES) never forget their first game. Gus Bodnar of Toronto will never forget the first 15 seconds of his first game in the National Hockey League against New York. That is how long it took for him to score a goal. No other rookie has ever scored quicker in his debut.

- The referee drops the puck between a designated member of each team.
  - The two players involved must have the blades of their sticks on the ice leaving enough room for the referee to drop the puck in between them.
  - Other players may not stand within 15 feet of the two players facing-off.
  - The two players involved in the face-off try to knock the puck to a teammate.

The team with possession of the puck attempts to advance it to an area where a player can strike (called SHOOT or PROPEL) the puck with his stick into the opponent's GOAL (over the goal line, between the goal posts, underneath the cross bar) for a score.

- A player may advance the puck toward a teammate by striking the puck with his stick, called PASSING.
- A player may advance the puck himself with his stick by pushing it along the ice while trying to out-maneuver the opponents, called STICKHANDLING.
  - The player "controlling" the puck is called the PUCK CARRIER.

After a team scores, a face-off takes place in the center of the rink.

If play has stopped, such as when the puck leaves the playing area, it is restarted with a face-off.

THE RINK

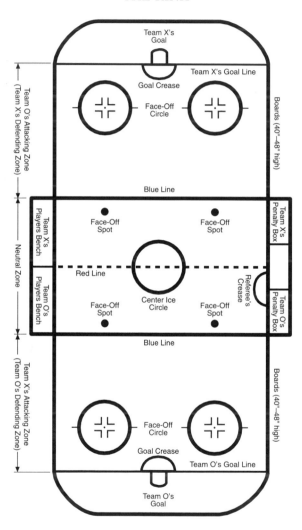

THE HOCKEY RINK

The standard rink is 200 feet long and 85 feet wide.
- Some rinks, including the one in Buffalo, are slightly smaller.
- The four corners are rounded.
- A fiberglass or wooden wall, called the BOARDS, surrounds the rink.
- The boards are between 40 to 48 inches high.
- Atop the boards is Plexiglas, usually just referred to as the GLASS.

Five lines stretch across the width of the ice.
- Two GOAL LINES 10 to 15 feet from each end of the ice.
    - Two GOAL POSTS are centered on each goal line, 6 feet apart.
        1. The goal posts are connected by a horizontal cross bar at a height of 4 feet.
        2. Attached to the goal posts and cross bar behind each goal line is a net to "catch" the puck when a goal is scored. The net plays no other significant role in the game.
            a. Remember that a goal is scored when the puck crosses entirely over the goal line underneath the cross bar. It does not have to touch the net.
        3. The goal posts are kept in place by flexible pegs inserted into the ice.

- One RED LINE at the center of the rink, that divides the rink in half lengthwise.
    - There is no red line in college hockey.
- Two BLUE LINES, 60 feet out from the goal lines.
    - Divide the ice between the goal lines into thirds.
        1. DEFENDING ZONE — The area from a

THE RINK

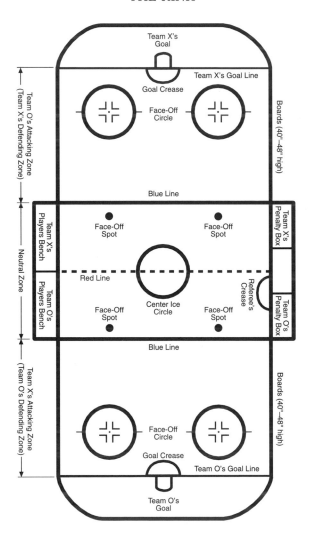

team's goal line to the closest blue line.

2. NEUTRAL ZONE — The area between the two blue lines.

3. ATTACKING ZONE or OFFENSIVE ZONE — The area between the furthest blue line to the opposing team's goal line.

   a. Important to remember that one team's attacking zone is the opposing team's defending zone and vice versa.

In front of each goal is a semicircle with a 6 foot radius, called the GOAL CREASE.

- The area of the ice enclosed by the goal crease is shaded with a light blue color to help the officials.

Five FACE-OFF CIRCLES, each with a radius of 15 feet, are drawn on the ice.

- One in the middle of the red line at CENTER ICE.
- Two in a team's defending zone, on each side of the goal.
- Two in a team's attacking zone, on each side of the goal.
- In the middle of each of the five face-off circles is a spot where a face-off takes place.

Four other face-off spots are on the ice in the neutral zone but without a circle.

- Each is located five feet from the nearest blue line.

Both team's PLAYERS' BENCHES are located behind the boards on the same side of the ice, where players sit when not playing.

- For the first period, the HOME TEAM will defend the goal closest to its players' bench. The VISITING TEAM will defend the other goal.
  - Teams switch sides between each of the periods.

THE RINK

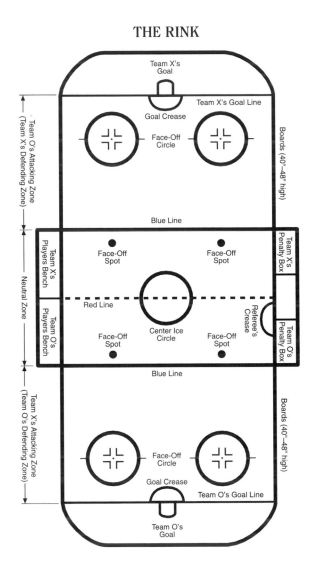

- The COACH usually stands behind the bench.
- Across each team's players' bench, behind the boards on the other side of the rink, is its PENALTY BENCH or PENALTY BOX.
    - Players must sit in this area when guilty of certain violations (discussed in detail later).
    - Broadcasters sometimes refer to it as the "sin bin."
    - On the ice in front of the area between the two penalty benches is a semicircle with a 10 foot radius, called the REFEREE'S CREASE.
        1. This area is off-limits to everyone but officials when play has stopped.
        2. The referee frequently retreats to his crease to discuss a violation with other officials without interference from arguing players.

Behind each goal at both ends of the rink are a red light and a green light.
- The red light indicates that a goal is scored.
- The green light indicates that a period is over.
    - The green light automatically prevents the red light from coming on, meaning once a period ends a goal cannot be scored.
    - If a player strikes the puck toward the opponent's net and the green light goes on before the puck crosses the goal line, the goal does not count.

GOALIE EQUIPMENT

Protective Mask

Blocking Glove
or Blocker

Catching Glove

Leg pad

Leg pad

Stick

THE PLAYERS

GOALIE, GOALKEEPER, GOALTENDER or NET MINDER—The player whose ultimate responsibility is to prevent the opposing team from scoring a goal.

- Positions himself in or near the goal crease.
- Wears the most equipment of all the players.
    - A protective mask.
    - Leg pads.
    - CATCHING GLOVE — Used to catch shots on goals.
    - A stick that has a wider blade and handle than the other players' sticks.
        1. BLOCKING GLOVE or BLOCKER — Used to hold the stick.
            a. The back of the glove is a rectangular padded area used to block shots.
- Usually will play the entire game without substitution, unless he is ineffective, giving up a number of goals.
- Many have the ability to do splits with their legs (OW!) to block the puck from going into the goal.
- Jacques Plante, who played in the 1950s and 1960s with the Montreal Canadiens, is one of the most famous goalies in hockey history.

Three FORWARDS or the FRONT LINE — The players who make up the front line of attack with an emphasis on scoring goals. Usually play 1 1/2 minutes at a time before being substituted.

- CENTER — Positioned in the middle of the line.
    - Closest to the opponent's goal, so usually is top scorer.
    - The player who controls the puck more than others because of his central position on the ice. He has more options to pass or shoot.
    - Must be an adept passer both forehanded and backhanded, passing the puck to the forwards on each side of him.

PLAYERS

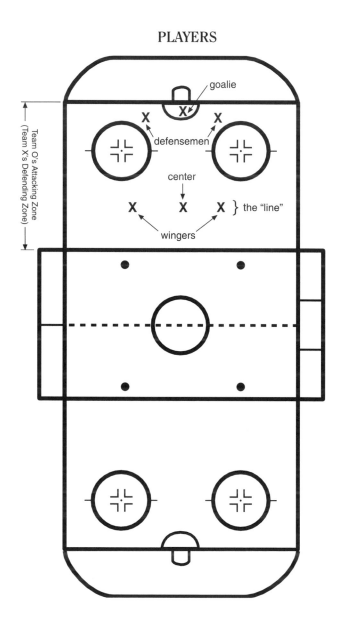

- Generally the player on the team who takes part in face-offs because of his experience in handling the puck.
- On defense, protects the area in the center of his defensive zone known as the SLOT.
- Two of the most famous centers are Wayne Gretzky and Mario Lemieux.

- TWO WINGS or WINGERS — Positioned on each side of the center.
  - Usually the left wing is left-handed or has a left-handed shot, while the right wing is right-handed or has a right-handed shot.
  - One wing often is more adept at scoring, while the other wing on the ice specializes in muscling with the opposition when the puck is in one of the corners of the rink.

    Two of the most famous wingers ever to play hockey were Gordie Howe and Bobby Hull.

- When not in the game, forwards sit on the end of the bench closest to its attacking zone.
  - When entering the game, are able to help out offensively more quickly.

TWO DEFENSEMEN — Positioned on each side of their goal to help the goalie prevent goals from being scored. Most of the time will play approximately 2 minutes before being substituted.

- Usually are defensive-minded but some are offensive-minded.
  - In the late 1960s, Bobby Orr was the first defenseman who emphasized scoring. He joined the forwards in the attack on the opponent's goal.
- On defense, one protects the left side of his defensive zone, the other protects the right side.
- Often larger than forwards so they can physically halt opponents onrushing toward their goal.
  - Also, can give out punishment by knocking opponents into the boards.
- Must be adept at skating backwards as they frequently

A defenseman, Arthur Brown, complained about the unfair media coverage players at his position receive: "All you newspaper guys want to talk about after a game are the scorers. You never come over to us to ask questions. But as soon as a goal is scored— boom, we get the blame."

• •

Milt Schmidt of the Boston Bruins was asked what he looks for when he signs defensemen for his team. He replied: "If they can fit through the door, I don't want 'em."

retreat to their defensive zone while keeping their eyes on the puck.

- When not in the game, will sit on the end of the bench closest to their defending zone.
  - When entering the game, are able to help out defensively more quickly.

CAPTAIN — One player selected by each team who can discuss with the referee questions regarding rules that may come up during the game.

- He wears a large "C" on the front of his jersey to identify himself as the captain.
- When the captain is not on the ice, an ALTERNATE CAPTAIN assumes his duties.
  - Each team can have no more than two alternate captains.
  - Each alternate captain wears a large "A" on the front of his jersey to identify himself.

Over the course of each game a team is allowed to play 18 players (not counting the goalies).

- Two goalies are dressed to play.
- If during the game both goalies are unable to continue playing, then a third may be used.

Before the game starts, the visiting team must disclose its starting lineup first.

- Some coaches will play their best defensive line against the opponent's top scoring line, sometimes called LINE MATCHING.

All players must wear a helmet.

- In the earlier days of hockey, wearing a helmet showed weakness of character. Now, safety is the priority.

Bernie "Boom Boom" Geoffrion, the colorful player and broadcaster, had one of the hardest slap shots in hockey history. Geoffrion earned his nickname because of the loud boom that would echo through the arena when one of his slap shots would hit the boards.

TERMS AND DEFINITIONS

PASS — A way to get the puck to a teammate such as:

- Scooping the puck up with the blade of the stick to lift it over an opponent's stick, skate or body.
- Leaving the puck for a teammate coming from behind, called a DROP PASS.
- Angling the puck toward the boards so that it will bounce off them to a teammate.
    - Effective when trying to get the puck around an opponent.
- Kicking the puck to a teammate.
- Slapping the puck with a hand to a teammate in his defending zone. This is called a HAND PASS or GLOVE PASS.
    - A player cannot intentionally hand pass the puck to a teammate who is in the neutral zone or in his attacking zone. Otherwise, play stops and a face-off takes place.
    - Why do the rules permit a hand pass between teammates in their *defensive zone*?
        a. Let's say a defenseman in his defending zone dropped his stick while the opponents were attacking. He might consider diving for a loose puck and slapping it to a nearby teammate forcing an official to stop play (and the opposing team's attack) because of the hand pass. The defenseman would then have time to retrieve his stick before play resumed with the face-off.
        b. To prevent the defenseman (or any other player) from benefiting by intentionally hand-passing the puck, the rules permit such a pass in his defensive zone.

SHOT — Attempt to score by striking the puck with a hockey stick toward the opponent's goal.

- SLAP SHOT — Player swings his stick back and then forward with great force, striking the puck.

"You don't have to be crazy to be a goaltender, but it helps." This is how the former goaltender of the Philadelphia Flyers, Bernie Parent, described his position.

- Puck comes off the stick like it was shot from a cannon, making it difficult for the opponent's goalie to block.
- Attempted when defenders are not nearby or else they could poke the puck away from the shooter.
- Often taken near the blue line of a team's attacking zone.

- WRIST SHOT — Player uses only his wrists in snapping the puck off his hockey stick.
    - Attempted when an offensive player is near the opponent's goal and has no time for a slap shot.

- FLIP SHOT — Puck is scooped up with the blade of the stick to lift it over an opponent's stick, skate or body toward the opponent's goal.
    - Occasionally done from the blue line of a team's attacking zone or even further back, hoping the crazy bounces off the ice will confuse the goalie.

- If a puck kicked or hand-batted by a player on the attacking team goes into an opponent's goal, it *does not* count as a score, even if it deflects off another player.

SHOT ON GOAL — A player on the attacking team shoots the puck toward the opponent's goal and it would go in if the goalie does not deflect it away.

- It is *not* a shot on goal if the goalie deflects the puck that would not have gone in the goal if he had let it go.

- It is *not* a shot on goal if a player hits the puck from his defending zone and it happens to go straight toward the opponent's goal before the goalie deflects it away.
    - If it is not an intended shot, it is not a shot on goal.

- It is *not* a shot on goal if the puck would have gone in the goal but someone on the defensive team, other than the goalie, deflects it away.

- It is *not* a shot on goal if the puck would have gone in but an offensive teammate who happens to be in the way, deflects it away.

GOALIE'S FIVE HOLE

The puck passing through the goalie's legs is said to have gone through the five hole.

- It is *not* a shot on goal if the puck strikes the goal posts, deflecting back away from the goal.

IN THE NETS or IN GOAL — Playing goalie.
- For example, a broadcaster will say, "Mike Richter is in the nets for the Rangers tonight."
- Sometimes called BETWEEN THE PIPES.

SHORT SIDE — When the goalie is not standing in the middle of the goal, the area between the goalie and the closest goal post to him.
- A broadcaster will describe a goal as, "Gretzky got it through the short side," letting the listening or viewing audience know that the puck was shot through the narrow opening.

SAVE — A goalie prevents an opponent's shot on goal from entering the goal either by stopping or deflecting the puck.
- KICK SAVE — Extending a leg or skate to block a shot.
- STICK SAVE — Using his stick to block a shot.
- GLOVE SAVE — Using his glove to block a shot.
- PAD SAVE — Blocking a shot with his protective leg pads.

FLOPPER — A goalie who freqently falls on the ice to block a shot.

FIVE HOLE — The space between the goalie's legs.
- After practicing for a while, goalies grow tired of constantly getting hit by the puck. Some coaches put a wooden board on the goal line with a picture of a goalie on it. The entire goal is covered except for the four corners numbered one through four and a space cut in between the "wooden goalie's" leg pads—the five hole.

REBOUND — Puck that bounces off the goal posts, cross bar, boards, opponent's goalie or another player after a shot is taken.

Some players' specialty is to score on power plays. During the 1966-67 season, Yvan Cournoyer of the Montreal Canadiens scored 25 goals and 20 of them came during power plays—80%.

- A rebounded puck in front of the opponent's goal is an excellent scoring opportunity.
- LOOSE PUCK — Puck not controlled by any player, usually after a rebound.

POWER PLAY — A team has more players on the ice than the opponents who have a player or players sitting in the penalty box.
- An excellent power play team scores a goal about 25% of the time or more.
- An average power play team scores a goal about 20% of the time.
- A poor power play team scores a goal about 15% of the time or less.

SHORT-HANDED — A team has fewer players on the ice than the opponents because of a penalty or penalties being SERVED in the penalty box by one or two of its players.
- Primary objective of a short-handed team is to use up as much time as possible until the penalty or penalties are over. This is called PENALTY KILLING.
    – An excellent penalty killing team does not allow a goal during a power play about 85% of the time.
    – An average penalty killing team does not allow a goal during a power play about 80% of the time.
    – A poor penalty killing team does not allow a goal during a power play about 75% of the time.
- It is a bonus when a short-handed team scores a goal, called a SHORT-HANDED GOAL, because it is concentrating on defense.

FULL STRENGTH—Team has six players on the ice.
- Broadcasters use this term when a player finishes serving his penalty and has entered the ice, ending the opponent's power play: "Lindros is out of the penalty box and now the Flyers are at full strength."

Harry Neale, the former coach of the Vancouver Canucks, complained: "Last season we couldn't win at home, and this season we can't win on the road. My failure as a coach is that I can't think of anyplace else to play."

FEED — A pass to a teammate who is in a position to score.

ASSIST — Credit given to a player who touches the puck immediately before a teammate scores.

- Credit for an assist is also given to a player who touches the puck immediately before a teammate touches the puck immediately before another teammate scores.
- If Player A passes the puck to Player B who shoots a goal, Player A is credited with an assist.
    - If Player C had passed the puck to Player A in the above example, Player C would also be given an assist.
- If Player A deflects Player B's shot into the opponent's goal for a score, Player A is credited with scoring the goal, while Player B is credited with an assist.
    - If Player C had passed the puck to Player B in the above example, Player C would also be given an assist.
- If Player A's shot rebounds off the goalie's stick and Player B knocks it into the goal, Player A is credited with an assist and Player B is credited with a goal.
    - If Player C had passed the puck to Player A in the above example, Player C would also be given an assist.
- No more than two assists can be awarded on each goal.
- A goal can be scored without an assist.
    - If a player steals the puck from an opponent and scores, it is an UNASSISTED goal—a teammate did not touch the puck before he scored the goal.

FREEZE — At least one player on each team gets tangled up, with the puck trapped against the boards.

SHIFT — Each time a player is on the ice until substituted.

Former coach of the Philadelphia Flyers, Fred Shero, had these words to say about his team's enforcer, Dave "the Hammer" Schultz: "There are three things that make a hockey player—speed, skill and strength. Schultz realizes that he does not have speed or skill, so what's he here for? To beat up the other guy, that's what."

● ●

After a hockey player scores a goal in a game, he may wonder what it will take to score two more for a hat trick. Bill Mosienko of the Chicago Blackhawks did not have time to wonder after he scored his first goal of the game against the New York Rangers on March 23, 1952. Mosienko scored two more goals in the next 21 seconds for his hat trick!

- Players want to play as many shifts as possible.

ENFORCER — A big, rugged player who ensures that his teammates are not treated roughly by the opposition.

BREAKAWAY — An offensive player has the puck while skating toward the opposing team's goal with only the goalie in between.

WRAPAROUND — The puck carrier who is behind the opponent's goal tries to curl his stick around to the front of the goal and knock the puck in.

DIG or MUCK — Attempt to gain possession of the puck that is in one of the corners of the ice.
- When opposing players are digging together, a lot of contact takes place.

FAN — To miss striking the puck on a pass or an attempted shot.

DEKE (short for decoy) — An offensive player fakes a move in one direction causing an opposing player to go in that direction. Frequently, this frees the offensive player to go a different way.
- Also refers to a player faking a pass in one direction and passing the puck in a different direction.

TOP SHELF — Upper portion of the goal, near the cross bar.
- A broadcaster frequently says, "He fooled the goal-keeper by shooting the puck in the top shelf."

SHUTOUT — A team does not allow the opposing team to score any goals during the game.

HAT TRICK — A player scores three goals in a game. Many fans respond after the third goal by throwing a hat on the rink. (Similar to the crowd throwing roses onto the ice after

LINESMEN

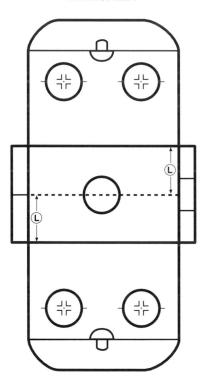

Each linesman moves between the center line and one of the blue lines.

an outstanding performance by a figure skater.)

- In the early days of hockey, a hat would be passed around the crowd to collect money for a 3-goal scorer.
- PURE HAT TRICK — A player scores three goals in a row during a game without a player on either team scoring in between.

STARS OF THE GAME — It is traditional that after every professional hockey game, the three players whose performances were judged the best by designated members of the media are recognized.

- Many fans do not leave the arena until they can pay tribute (by applause) to the stars of the game whose names are announced to the crowd.
- Often at least one home team player is a star of the game, even if the home team loses.

COACH — Directs the actions of his team on the ice.

- Generally has one or more assistants who specialize as a goalie coach, or a special teams coach focusing on power plays and penalty-killing.

REFEREE — Responsible for both teams obeying the rules of the game.

- The man in charge.
- Drops the puck during face-offs at the beginning of each period and after a goal is scored.
- Wears an orange armband on each sleeve to easily distinguish him from the other officials.
- Stops play when he is not able to see the puck on the ice (a face-off follows).
- May use television replays to review when a goal is disputed.

LINESMEN — The two officials who assist the referee on the ice.

- Primary responsibility is to ensure that the icing and off-side rules are not violated (discussed in detail later).
- Drop the puck during face-offs except at the

The home team used to ensure that
one of the goal's nets was drawn very tight.
Hometown goal judges would not allow a goal when
the puck banged in and out of the net. Cleverly,
home teams would choose to defend the goal with
the tight net two of the three periods.

beginning of each period and after a goal is scored.
- Break up "physical disputes" between opposing players.

GOAL JUDGES — The two officials who determine if the entire puck goes beyond the goal line between the goal posts for a goal.
- Positioned in back of each goal behind the boards.
- Turns on switch connected to a red light at both ends of the rink behind each goal, when he determines that a goal is scored.
    - The referee makes the final decision whether a disputed goal is scored.

VIDEO GOAL JUDGE — Uses the replays on a TV monitor to determine if a goal is valid.
    - For example, makes sure the puck wasn't kicked into the goal, or didn't cross the goal line after the end of a period.
    - Also, only if the referee asks, checks whether an attacking player was illegally in the goal crease when the puck crossed the goal line. (see Interference)

OFF-SIDES

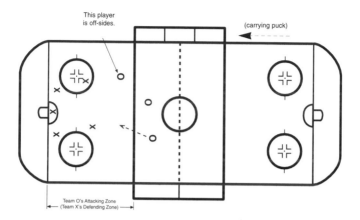

Play is stopped for off-sides because a player was already in his attacking zone when a teammate carried the puck into that zone.

DELAYED OFF-SIDES

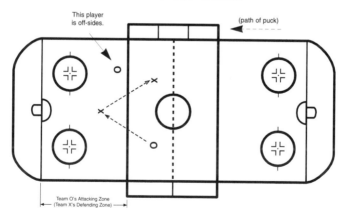

Play is not stopped for off-sides even though a player is already in his attacking zone when a teammate hits the puck into that zone. A defending player intercepted the puck and passed it out of the zone. If an attacking player had touched the puck inside the zone, off-sides would have been called.

THREE KEY VIOLATIONS

OFF-SIDES — A player is already in his attacking zone when the puck enters that zone and the puck is touched by that player or a teammate.

- A player is considered in his attacking zone when both of his skates are entirely across the blue line.

- During a game, watch how players of the attacking team will straddle or stand behind the blue line in front of their attacking zone, waiting for a teammate to pass or carry the puck across that blue line.

- Off-sides is never called on the player who is controlling the puck (even if his skates are in his attacking zone while the puck he is controlling is still behind the blue line).

- After off-sides is called, a face-off takes place in the neutral zone at the face-off spot closest to the guilty team's attacking zone.

- DELAYED OFF-SIDES — A player is already in his attacking zone when the puck enters that zone, but the puck is not yet touched by the player or a teammate. Off-sides is not immediately whistled by a linesman. He waits to see how the action further develops.

  - Off-sides will not be called if the off-side player or a teammate does not touch the puck until the puck is intercepted by an opponent who carries the puck or passes the puck into the neutral zone. Otherwise, off-sides will be called (which is why it is called delayed off-sides).

  - If the team with the off-sides player does not gain an advantage, officials do not want to "penalize" the opposing team who ended up with control of the puck, by stopping play for a face-off. The rules say, "Let the play continue."

  - In a delayed off-side situation, the linesman raises his hand but does not blow his whistle

43

OFF-SIDES PASS (OR TWO-LINE PASS)

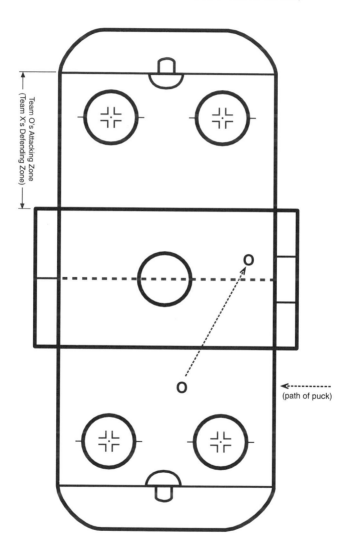

A player passes the puck from his defending zone
(crossing two lines) to a teammate who is already
beyond the center line.

to stop play. He waits to see if off-sides must eventually be called as discussed above. If off-sides is no longer applicable, the linesman gives the WASH-OUT signal.

1. He swings his arms at shoulder level with his palms down.

- If a player carries the puck back into his defending zone while an opposing player is already in that zone, off-sides is not called on that opposing player.

  – Yes, the opposing player was in his attacking zone before the puck got there (the criteria for off-sides), but since his team did not have control of the puck, the rules say, "Let the play continue."

- If a puck deflects off a defender in the neutral zone and it goes back into his defending zone while an opposing player is already in that zone, off-sides is not called on that opposing player.

  – Yes, the opposing player was in his attacking-zone before the puck got there (the criteria for off-sides), but since his team did not "cause" the puck to go back in his attacking zone, the rules say, "Let the play continue."

- The purpose of the off-sides rule is to prevent players from "loitering" near the goal, waiting for a pass from a teammate—especially when the action is in the neutral zone or their defending zone.

OFF-SIDES PASS or TWO-LINE PASS — A player in his defending zone passes the puck forward to a teammate and the puck crosses both the blue line and the red line.

- It is not an off-sides pass if the puck crossed the red line before the teammate receiving the pass.

- If an off-sides pass is called, a face-off takes place from where the pass was made.

ICING THE PUCK or ICING — A player knocks the puck from his half of the ice across the red line and the opponent's goal line and the puck is first touched by an

ICING

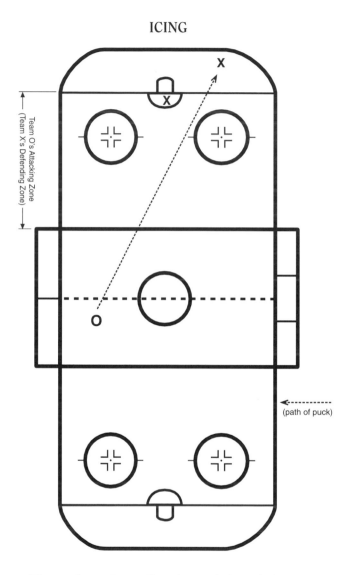

The puck-carrier strikes the puck from behind the center line and it is touched by an opponent (other than the goalie) after it crosses the goal line.

opponent (other than the goalie).

- It is not icing the puck if:
    - A team has less players on the ice than the opposing team (an opponent's power play).
    - The puck goes into the opponent's goal.
    - The puck passes through the goal crease before it reaches the goal line.
    - The puck touches any part of an opponent before it reaches the goal line.
    - The puck goes beyond the goal line directly from a face-off.
    - A player of the opposing team is able to touch the puck before it crosses his goal line but decides not to touch it.
    - The opposing team's goalie touches the puck either before or after the puck crosses the goal line.

- If icing is not called because of one of the exceptions above, the linesman will give the wash-out signal (the same signal discussed previously when there is no off-sides).
- After icing is called, a face-off takes place in the defending zone of the team that iced the puck.
- The opposing team's goalie will signal his teammate who is racing for the puck that the linesman will call icing once he touches the puck (called the TOUCH UP).
- The rule disallowing icing was necessary so that the game did not turn into a boring exercise of teams knocking the puck from one end of the rink to the other.

The rules in hockey specifically state that the doors leading from the players' benches and penalty benches to the ice must only swing away from the ice. In the 1940s, Detroit's Olympia had doors that swung toward the ice. Imagine the injuries that took place in that arena.

PENALTIES

Officials punish players and their teams with penalties
if they violate certain rules (discussed in detail later),
especially those involving illegal contact with an
opponent.

The types of penalties include:

- MINOR PENALTY — Given to a player who breaks a
  rule while playing on the ice. The guilty player, other
  than the goalkeeper, must leave the ice and go to the
  penalty box for two minutes.
    - During the two minutes, the player may not be
      substituted for on the ice. His team must play
      with one less player.
        1. Once the two minutes expire, the player
           may immediately enter the ice.
    - If the goalkeeper is guilty, a teammate who was
      on the ice when the rule was broken serves the
      two minutes in the penalty box.
        1. The player is chosen by the coach.
        2. That same player must stay in the
           penalty box for the entire two minutes.
           He may not be replaced in the penalty
           box by another teammate.
    - If a team is short-handed because one of its
      players is serving a minor penalty, the player
      may return to the ice before the two minutes
      expire if the other team scores.
        1. If a team is short-handed by two
           players because two of its players are
           serving minor penalties, the person who
           incurred the first penalty may return to
           the ice before the two minutes expire if
           the other team scores.
    - COINCIDENTAL MINOR PENALTIES — At the
      same time, minor penalties are called against
      an equal number of players on each team.
        1. If coincidental minor penalties are
           assessed against one player on each
           team at a time when no other players

In the early days of hockey, there used to be just one penalty box and it was used by both teams. Think about players being sent to the same penalty box for fighting on the ice. More enforcers than players used to occupy the penalty box.

are serving penalties, both teams play with one less player on the ice for the two minutes.

    a. So, if both penalty boxes are empty and the referee calls coincidental minor penalties on one player on each team, the teams resume playing with five players on the ice for each team.

  2. If coincidental minor penalties are assessed against more than one player on each team or if other players are already serving penalties when the coincidental minor penalties are called, the teams may substitute for the penalized players.

- BENCH MINOR PENALTY — Given to a team as a result of breaking one of the rules while not on the ice, such as a coach verbally abusing an official.

  - Any player on the team (except a goalkeeper) can be chosen by his coach to sit in the penalty box for two minutes because of the bench minor penalty.

  - All other rules of a normal minor penalty apply, such as if the team is short-handed and it gives up a goal, the bench minor penalty automatically ends.

- MAJOR PENALTY — Given to a player who in the judgment of the referee has severely violated a rule while playing on the ice. The guilty player, other than the goalkeeper, must leave the ice and go to the penalty box for five minutes.

  - During the five minutes, the player may not be substituted for on the ice. His team must play with one less player.

    1. Once the five minutes expire, the player may immediately enter the ice.

  - If the goalkeeper is guilty, a teammate who was on the ice when the rule was broken serves the five minutes in the penalty box.

    1. The player is chosen by the coach.

    2. That same player must stay in the

Former NHL referee, Bill Chadwick, called a holding penalty on the Chicago Blackhawks Johnny Mariucci, in a game against the Minnesota North Stars. Mariucci protested causing the hometown Chicago fans to howl. One of the fans dropped a deck of cards on the ice. Mariucci continued to complain, Chadwick picked up the deck, gave it to him and said, "Here John, you can use these for a game of solitaire because you just got ten more minutes for misconduct."

penalty box for the entire five minutes. He may not be replaced in the penalty box by another teammate.

- If a team is short-handed because one of its players is serving a major penalty, the player must stay in the penalty box until the entire five minutes expire, even if the other team scores.

    1. Remember that a goal scored when a team is short-handed because of a minor penalty enables the penalized player to immediately enter the ice. A major penalty is more severe to match the severity of the violation.

- COINCIDENTAL MAJOR PENALTIES — At the same time, major penalties are called against an equal number of players on each team.

    1. The teams may substitute for the penalized players.

    2. When the penalties expire, the penalized players may not enter the ice immediately. They must wait until there is a face-off (a stop in the action) so that their substitutes can leave the ice.

● MISCONDUCT PENALTY — Given to a player who acts in an unsportsmanlike manner. The guilty player, other than the goalkeeper, must leave the ice and go to the penalty box for ten minutes.

- During the ten minutes the player may be substituted for on the ice. His team does not have to play with one less player. (Note how this differs from a minor and a major penalty in which the penalized team must play with one less player.)

- If the goalkeeper is guilty, a teammate who was on the ice when the rule was broken serves the ten minutes in the penalty box.

    1. The player is chosen by the coach.

    2. That same player must stay in the penalty box for the entire ten minutes. He may not be replaced in the penalty box by another teammate.

Rodney Dangerfield's famous one-liner in 1978:
"I went to a fight the other night and a
hockey game broke out."

- When the ten minutes expire, the penalized-player may not enter the ice immediately. He must wait until there is a face-off (a stop in the action).

- GAME MISCONDUCT PENALTY — Given to a player (including the goalkeeper) who in the referee's judgement has acted in such an unsportsmanlike manner that he no longer is eligible to play for the remainder of the game.

  - Just like a regular misconduct penalty, the penalized player may be substituted for on the ice. His team does not have to play with one less player for the remainder of the game.

  - Automatically given to a player upon receiving his third major penalty in the same game.

  - Automatically given to a player upon receiving a major penalty for one of the following offenses (discussed in detail later):

    1. Butt-ending
    2. Cross-checking
    3. High-sticking
    4. Slashing
    5. Spearing
    6. Checking from behind
    7. Clipping

- MATCH PENALTY — Given to a player (including the goalkeeper) who in the referee's judgment has played in such a dangerous manner that he no longer is eligible to play for the remainder of the game.

  - The penalized player may be substituted for after five minutes. During the five minutes, his team must play with one less player.

- PENALTY SHOT — Awarded to the opponents when a player intentionally commits a violation to prevent a possible goal.

  - The fouled player, in most cases, is given possession of the puck at the center red line.

  - The opposing team's goalie must stay in his crease until the player taking the penalty shot touches the puck.

Dentists love to have hockey players as patients. A survey was once taken that indicated 68 percent of all players in the National Hockey League have lost at least one tooth during a game.

- All other players on the ice must stand on the sides in front of their players' bench until the penalty shot is attempted.
- At the referee's signal, the fouled player skates toward the goal with the puck.
  1. Once he crosses the attacking blue line, the puck must be in constant motion toward the opponent's goal (he cannot skate backwards with the puck).
  2. When he shoots, the goalie tries to block the shot.
  3. If the puck goes into the goal, a goal is scored. If it does not, the penalty shot ends and regular play is restarted with a face-off.
     a. During a penalty shot, a player does not get a second chance to knock the puck into the goal if his original shot rebounded back to him.
- Statistics show that approximately 30% of attempted penalty shots have been successful.

If a team already has two players serving penalties and a third player incurs a penalty:
- The third player must proceed to the penalty box.
- A substitute for the third player may enter the ice.
  - No matter how many penalties a team incurs, it must be allowed to play with three players plus a goalie.
- The third player's penalty time does not start running until the first player is allowed back on the ice.
  - At the face-off (stop in the action) following the expiration of the first player's penalty time (or if the opposing team scores a power play goal and the first player is serving a minor penalty):
    1. The first player serving a penalty can enter the ice.
    2. The substitute for the third player must go to his players' bench.
    3. The third player's penalty time starts ticking away.

In a 1983 game between the home team
NY Islanders and the Edmonton Oilers, the crowd
went berserk when referee Ron Hoggarth called
three penalties in a row against the Islanders.
Denis Potvin, the Islander captain, skated up to
him and asked, "Hey Hoggarth, how can
you sleep through this noise?"

If a penalty is called on a team that has possession of the puck, the referee blows his whistle ending the play.

If a penalty is called on a team that does not have possession of the puck, the referee signals that there is a penalty but does not blow his whistle (called a DELAYED PENALTY), allowing play to continue.

- Play stops (and the referee blows his whistle) once the penalized team gains control again of the puck or if there is a face-off.

- If the fouled team scores before play stops, a minor penalty does not have to be served. By giving up the goal, the penalized team has suffered enough.

  - Similar to a power play when a minor penalty ends if the fouled team scores.

- If the fouled team scores before play stops, a major or match penalty still does have to be served. This illustrates the severity of a major or match penalty, compared to a minor penalty.

  - Similar to a power play when a major or match penalty continues even if the fouled team scores.

Stan Mikita, the former center with the
Chicago Blackhawks, made the following interesting
comment: "There are rough players and there
are dirty players. I'm rough and dirty."

MORE VIOLATIONS

BOARDING — Making contact with an opponent forcing him to crash dangerously into the boards.

- The result is a minor or major penalty depending on how severe the contact was. It is up to the referee's judgment.
- The result is a major and a game misconduct penalty if the contact resulted in an injury to the head or face of an opponent.

CHARGING — A player violently makes contact with an opponent, but not into the boards.

- The result is a minor or major penalty depending on how severe the contact was. It is up to the referee's judgment.

CHECKING FROM BEHIND — Making contact with an opponent on the back part of his body. This is a dangerous violation because the opponent is unable to defend himself.

- The result is a major and a game misconduct penalty.

CLIPPING — Making contact with an opponent on or below his knees.

- The result is a minor penalty.
- If an injury occurs a major and game misconduct is assessed.

INTERFERENCE — A player is guilty of defensive interference if he uses his body to make contact with an opponent who does not have the puck or did not just have the puck. A player is guilty of offensive interference if he purposely gets in the way of a defender, causing contact.

- The result is a minor penalty.
- Interference is called if a player makes contact with the goalkeeper that could have been avoided.
- If a player intentionally knocks an opponent's stick out of his hand or prevents him from picking it up, it is interference.

Bill "Cowboy" Fleet was a winger
on the Philadelphia Flyers during the 1970s.
Intimidation was his specialty. He would whisper
to the opposing team's rookies: "The first time you
touch the puck, I'll break your arm."

- If an attacking player (or his stick) is in the opponent's goal crease when the puck is not in the crease, and the puck goes into the goal, the score does not count and interference is called.

ROUGHING — A player strikes an opponent but not in a way that would cause a major altercation.
- The result is one minor penalty.

ELBOWING   A player uses his elbow in making contact with an opponent.
- The result is a minor or major penalty as determined by the referee. If the fouls results in injury, the referee may also issue a game misconduct.

KNEEING — A player makes contact with an opponent using his knee.
- The result is a minor, major or match penalty as determined by the referee.

HEAD-BUTTING — A player intentionally makes or attempts to make contact with an opponent using his helmet.
- The result is a double minor if no contact is made.
- A major and a game misconduct results if contact is made.
- A match penalty is issued if the player's helmet caused injury to the opponent.

TRIPPING — Player moves his leg, arm, knee or stick into a position that causes an opponent to trip.
- The result is a minor penalty.
- If the tripping is caused by a player successfully HOOK CHECKING (discussed in detail later) the puck from an opponent, no penalty is called.

KICKING A PLAYER — A player kicks or attempts to kick an opposing player.
- The result is a match penalty.

Former Philadelphia Flyer, Dave "the Hammer" Schultz, was being heckled by a teen-age boy during a game. Schultz swung his stick at him just missing the boy's fingers. The boy's mother screamed, "You should be ashamed of yourself." Schultz yelled back, "I'll get you too, lady."

The next game, the boy was there again with his father. Schultz swore at him and squirted him with water from a plastic bottle.

HOLDING — A player holds an opponent with his hands or his hockey stick. He also cannot hold an opponent's stick with his hands.

- The result is a minor penalty.

HOOKING — Player uses the curved portion of a hockey stick's blade to hold an opponent.

- The result is a minor penalty.
- If an opponent suffers an injury as a result of hooking, the result is a major penalty and game misconduct.

CROSS-CHECKING — While holding the stick with both hands and arms extended (and the stick not touching the ice), a player's stick makes contact with an opponent.

- The result is a minor or major (along with a game misconduct) penalty depending how severe the contact was. It is up to the referee's judgment.

BUTT-ENDING — A player attempts or actually makes contact with an opponent by jabbing the gripped-end of the stick into him.

- The result is a double minor if no contact is made.
- A major and a game misconduct results if contact is made.
- A match penalty is issued if the player's helmet caused injury to the opponent.

HIGH-STICKING — Player carries his stick above the height of his opponent's shoulders and makes contact.

- The referee can assess either a minor, two minors or a major penalty.
- If the high sticking caused injury to an opponent:
    - And it was accidental, two minor penalties are the result.
    - And it was flagrant, a match penalty results.
- High-sticking is also called if a player bats the puck with his stick when it is above his shoulders.
    - The result is a face-off, unless the puck is batted to an opponent. In that case, play continues.

Gordie Howe, who earned his fame as a Detroit Red Wing winger, was asked if he had ever broken his nose. He replied, "No, but 11 other guys did."

- If a player bats the puck into the goal with his stick carried above the height of the cross bar, the score is not allowed.

SLASHING — Player swings his stick at an opponent even if contact is not made.
- The referee can assess either a minor or a major penalty and game misconduct.
- The result is a major and a game misconduct penalty if an opponent is injured.

SPEARING — A player attempts or actually makes contact with an opponent by stabbing the end of the stick's blade into him.
- The result is a double minor if no contact is made.
- A major and a game misconduct results if contact is made.
- A match penalty is issued if the player's helmet caused injury to the opponent.

FIGHTS — A player may not participate in a fight with the opposition.
- The result is a major penalty.
- The referee can also assess a minor, another major or a game misconduct penalty.
  - A player who intentionally removes his sweater before engaging in a fight is automatically given a minor penalty and a game misconduct.
- All players not involved in the fight must go to a neutral area such as their players' bench.
  - The first player to join a fight between two opposing players (and becomes the THIRD MAN IN) can be given a game misconduct by the referee.
  - The first player to leave either the players' bench or the penalty box to join a fight not only receives a game misconduct penalty, but also is automatically suspended for the next 10 games.
  - The second player to leave either the players'

Gordie Howe skated over to referee Frank Udvari during a game and said: "Frank, you're the second-best referee." Udvari was a bit flattered and asked, "Well, who's the best?" Howe replied: "Everyone else. They're tied for number one."

bench or the penalty box to join a fight not only receives a game misconduct penalty, but also is automatically suspended for the next 5 games.

● If a player starts a fight, he is given a minor, a major and a misconduct penalty.

—A player is suspended for 10 games if he starts a fight before a period begins or after a period ends.

● If a player is hit by an opponent and retaliates by swinging back at him, he is given a minor penalty.

—A double minor, major or a game misconduct is assessed if the player continues to retaliate.

ATTEMPT TO INJURE — A player attempts to injure an opposing player regardless if the attempt to injure is successful.

● The result is a match penalty.

● A substitute is allowed for the guilty player after five minutes have passed. His team must play short-handed for that amount of time.

DELAYING THE GAME — A player intentionally bats or shoots the puck over the boards.

● The result is a minor penalty.

● If the goalkeeper shoots the puck directly (without it being deflected) over the glass into the stands, he is given a minor penalty even if it was not intentional.

BROKEN STICK — A player, other than the goalie, may not continue to play while holding a stick that is broken.

● He must drop the broken stick or he will be given a minor penalty.

● A player must go to his players' bench for another stick that has to be handed, not thrown, to him.

● A player may receive a stick from a teammate but that teammate must go to his players' bench for a replacement.

● Goalies have different rules with regard to broken sticks.

– May continue playing with a broken stick until

Toe Blake, a former star with the Montreal Canadiens, was given a two-minute penalty by referee Mickey Ion during a game. Blake's angry response was: "I don't want to get another penalty, but you can guess what I'm thinking." Ion replied: "I have guessed—and you get another five minutes."

the next face-off or until they are given a stick by a teammate.

- May not go to his players' bench for a replacement or he will be given a minor penalty.

HANDLING PUCK WITH HANDS — A player, other than a goalie, may not close his hand on the puck or he will be given a minor penalty.

- A player is permitted to stop or direct the puck in the air with his open hand or push it along the ice.
  - Remember he cannot intentionally slap the puck with his hand to a teammate who is not in his defending zone.
  - If a player on the attacking team slaps the puck with his hand and the puck directly goes into an opponent's goal, it does not count as a score.
  - If a player on the attacking team slaps the puck with his hand and it deflects off an opponent (other than the goalie) and goes into an opponent's goal, it does not count as a score.
- A player, except the goalie, may not pick up the puck from the ice with his hand or he will be given a minor penalty.
  - If he picks it up in his team's goal crease, the opposing team is awarded a penalty shot.
- A goalie may not hold the puck with his hands for longer than three seconds (unless he is being checked by an opponent) or he will be given a minor penalty.
- A goalie may not throw the puck toward the opponent's goal or he will be given a minor penalty.
  - If an opposing player controls the thrown puck, the referee signals that there is a penalty but does not blow his whistle, allowing play to continue.
    1. Play stops (and the referee blows his whistle) once the penalized team gains control again of the puck or if there is a face-off.
    2. If the opposing team scores before play stops, the minor penalty does not have to be served.

An appreciation for the unique and
rowdy character of the game of hockey can be
learned from the cult hit movie *Slap Shot*.

FALLING ON PUCK — A player may not intentionally fall on the puck or pull the puck into his body.

- The result is a minor penalty.
- The result is a penalty shot if the violation is by a player on the defending team (other than the goal-keeper) in his goal crease.
    - A goalkeeper is not guilty of this infraction in the goal crease if opposing players are near him.

ARGUING WITH AN OFFICIAL — A player may not argue with an official about a ruling.

- The result is a minor penalty.
- If the player continues arguing, he could receive a misconduct and a game misconduct penalty.

DIVING — A player may not fake receiving contact from another player.

- The result is a minor penalty.

SPECIAL RULES

1. While in the opponent's half of the ice, if a player is fouled from behind and only the goalkeeper is between him and the goal, a penalty shot is awarded once the guilty team gains possession of the puck.

2. While in the opponents' half of the ice, if a player is fouled from behind with the opposing team's goalkeeper pulled (discussed in detail later) and no opponent between the player and the goal, a goal is awarded to the attacking team.

SCREEN THE GOALIE

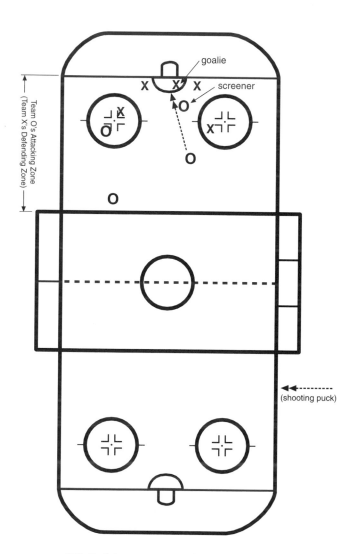

While his teammate shoots the puck,
an attacking player stands outside of the goal
crease blocking the goalie's line of sight.

COMMON OFFENSIVE STRATEGIES

CENTER LEADS ATTACK — The center tries to control the puck over his attacking zone's blue line. If he cannot:

- He looks for a winger who can receive a pass.
- He DUMPS THE PUCK into the attacking zone and often races with a winger toward the rebound off the boards.
    - The first one to get there goes after the defender.
    - The second one to get there goes after the puck.
    - The other winger positions himself in the SLOT (approximately half-way between the goal crease and the center of the blue line) awaiting a pass.
    - Sometimes the puck is dumped into the attacking zone to give the team a chance to change on the fly and substitute its players.
- He shoots at the goal. Even if the puck does not go in the goal, it might bounce off the goalie for an easy shot.

GOALIE'S STICK SIDE   Most attacking players prefer to shoot the puck toward the part of the net closest to the goalie's stick rather than on the other side closest to his glove. Here's why:

- Goalies usually move their stick slower than their glove to block a shot.
- If the puck hits the stick it could easily bounce off creating an opportunity for another shot at close range.

SCREEN THE GOALIE — A forward stands just outside of the opponent's goal crease in an attempt to block the view of the goalie during a teammate's shot on goal.

- Even if the goalie is able to block the shot, the forward is in position to hit the rebounded puck into the goal.

Jacques Plante summarized life as a goaltender for the Montreal Canadiens as follows: "How would you like it if you were sitting in your office and you made one little mistake—suddenly, a big red light went on behind you and 18,000 people jumped up and started screaming at you, calling you a bum and an imbecile. Then they started throwing a lot of garbage at you. Well, that's what it's like when you play goal for a team in the NHL."

CENTER THE PUCK — A player close to the boards in his attacking zone passes the puck into or near the goal crease, with the intent of creating an opportunity for a teammate to score.

DEFENSEMAN ON ATTACK — Frequently sets up at a POINT (just within the attacking zone near the boards) to help keep the puck in the attacking zone.
- If the puck leaves a team's attacking zone into the neutral zone, all players on the offensive team will skate out of their attacking zone to avoid being offsides.
    - To help defensively.
    - To avoid an off-sides violation.
        1. If a player was in his attacking zone while the puck was in the neutral zone where a teammate gained possession of the puck, what would happen next?
        a. If the player stayed in the attacking zone when the puck entered that zone—off-sides would be called. To avoid the violation, his teammate would have to wait for the player to skate behind the blue line before the puck could enter the attacking zone. This delay would give the opponents more time to set up defensively.

POWER PLAY — Teams play their best offensive players on the power play to increase the chances of scoring while they outnumber their opponents on the ice.
- Some teams use four forwards and one defenseman to put more pressure on the short-handed opponents.
    - The risk in not having two defensemen is not great because the emphasis of the short-handed opponents is to kill penalties, not to try to score.

PULL THE GOALIE — A team's goalie is taken out of the game and replaced by a forward in the following situations:
- A delayed penalty is being called on the opponents.

How can a goalie score a goal for his team? It happened on November 28, 1979 in a game between the Colorado Rockies and the New York Islanders. A penalty was called against the Islanders, but the Rockies had control of the puck, so play continued.

The Rockies pulled their goalie, but it cost them. Colorado forward, Rob Ramage, got to the puck after it was blocked by Islander goalie, Billy Smith. From behind the goal line, Ramage tried to pass it to a teammate near his team's attacking zone's blue line, but it went all the way down the ice into his team's empty goal.

Islander goalie, Billy Smith, was credited with the goal because he was the last Islander to touch the puck before it went into the Rockies' goal.

- There is no risk in removing the goalie and leaving the goal unattended because play stops once the team that is penalized controls the puck. As long as the fouled team controls the puck, play continues.
- Puts more pressure on the opponents with an extra attacker trying to score.
- The fouled team's goalie races toward his team's players' bench once he sees a penalty called against the opponents and a forward will jump over the boards when the goalie is within five feet of the players' bench. Watch for it next time!

● A team is losing late in the third period and the puck is controlled by the team in its attacking zone.

- In the little time remaining, it wants to increase its chances of scoring and tying the game with a man advantage in the attacking zone.
- The risk is the opposing team could intercept a pass and shoot the puck into the empty net (known, not surprisingly, as an EMPTY-NET GOAL) for a bigger lead.
  1. Losing by one goal or two is still losing, so a team behind in the score might as well take the chance at tying the game and sending it into sudden-death overtime.
- If a team pulls its goalie, and then a face-off is to take place in the team's defending zone, the goalie will come back on the ice.
  1. When the puck is once again controlled by his team in the neutral zone, he'll come off the ice another time.

DEKING — The puck carrier fakes a shot and while a defender is preparing to block it, he skates by.

CREATE TRIANGLES — Two offensive players position themselves so that a triangle is created with the teammate who has the puck.

● Makes it difficult for defenders to anticipate where the puck is going.

BREAKAWAY — On a breakaway, it is better to skate in the middle so there are two sides of the net to shoot at instead of one (if he were to skate down one of the sides).

GIVE AND GO — An offensive player passes ("gives") the puck and then skates ("goes") toward the opponent's goal, anticipating a return pass for an easy shot.

- The defender tends to follow the puck as it is passed, taking his attention away from the offensive player who passed it.
- The offensive player gets away from the defender during the momentary lapse and is open to receive the return pass.

CLEAR THE ZONE

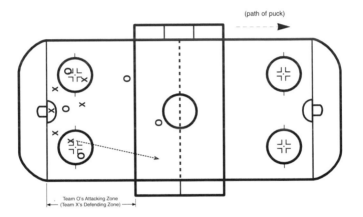

A defensive player in his defending zone clears
the puck out of the zone, forcing the opponents
to come out of the zone before their next
attack to avoid off-sides.

COMMON DEFENSIVE STRATEGIES

CLEAR THE PUCK — A defender moves the puck away from a dangerous situation (usually when the puck is in front of the goal he is defending) as quickly as possible.

- It is even better if the defender clears the puck out of his defending zone (sometimes called CLEAR THE ZONE).
    - Forces all the opposing players to go behind the blue line into the neutral zone before its next attack on goal.
        1. If the opponents do not go behind the blue line, when the puck comes back into the opponents' attacking zone, they will be ahead of the puck and off-side will be called.
- The attacking team tries to "hold it in," which means keep the puck in the zone so that all of its players do not have to go behind the blue line before its next attack on goal.

PENALTY KILLING — Ways that a short-handed team tries to use up time until it returns to full strength.

- A BOX DEFENSE is frequently used.
    - Two forwards are used and they each position themselves between the opposing team's wing and the slot.
    - The other two players stand on each side of the goal.
    - If a team has two fewer players on the ice than the opponents, a TRIANGLE DEFENSE is used.
        1. One forward is used and he moves from one side of the slot to the other, depending on where the puck is.
        2. The other two players stand near the goal.
- Clear the puck out of the defensive zone by shooting it over the nearby blue line.
    - It is even better to ice the puck (shoot it all the

"Forecheck, backcheck and paycheck." This is how the great center of the Buffalo Sabres, Gil Perreault, responded when asked what were the three most important parts of hockey.

way down the ice over the opposing team's goal line) because that kills more time (which is why the term PENALTY KILLING is used).

> 1. Remember it is legal for a short-handed team to ice the puck.

- Try to maintain possession of the puck when it is out of its defending zone.

LINE MATCHING — A coach may insert into the game his best defensive line against the opponents' top scoring line.

BODY CHECKING — Making contact with an opponent primarily using one's shoulder or arm.

- Usually done while an opponent is concentrating on receiving or passing the puck.
- Not allowed in college hockey by a player in his attacking zone.

HIP CHECKING — Making contact with an opponent using one's hips.

- Usually done into the boards as an opponent is about to slip away.

STICK CHECKING — Taking the puck away from an opponent using one's hockey stick.

- POKE CHECK — A defensive player lunges toward an opponent who has the puck, brushing his stick against his opponent's, poking the puck loose.
  - Cannot trip an opponent while poke checking.
- SWEEP CHECK — In a circular motion, a defensive player tries to sweep the puck away from an opponent.
- HOOK CHECK — A defensive player turns the blade of his stick inward to form a hook and tries to get the blade in front of the puck as it comes off the opponent's stick.

FORECHECKING — Usually a forward harrassing opponents in the opponents' defensive zone.

- Especially effective behind the net where the

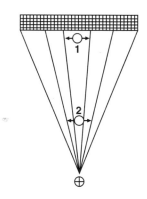

CUT DOWN THE ANGLE

The scoring angle is reduced
by the goalkeeper moving
from position 1
to position 2.

opposing player with the puck has less room to maneuver.

- Poke checking and hook checking are used.
- Gives fellow teammates time to set up defensively.

BACK-CHECKING — Usually a forward helping out his defensemen by harrassing opponents in the opponents' attacking zone.

- Constantly keeping the stick moving—poke checking, making it difficult for an opposing player to pass, shoot or receive a pass.

CUT DOWN THE ANGLE — The goalie skates out from the crease toward an opponent onrushing with the puck.

- The opponent sees less of the goal than if the goalie stayed in the crease.
- As the goalie approaches the puck carrier, the margin of a potential scoring shot (that will get between the goalie and one of the goal posts) is geometrically reduced.
  - To illustrate, form a triangle (with the goal line as the base) by drawing a line from the puck carrier to each goal post. Put the goalie on the goal line.
  - From the puck carrier's perspective, note the substantial amount of space ("wide angles") between the goalkeeper and each goal post. As the goalkeeper (with outstretched arms) comes closer to the puck carrier, these spaces become smaller, thus cutting down the angle of the puck carrier's opportunities.
  - This strategy can be risky. With the goalie out of position, the defending team is vulnerable to the puck carrier:
    1. Skating around the goalie.
    2. Passing to a teammate.
    3. Shooting at the goalie, hoping for a rebound to himself or to another offensive player with a clear shot to the goal.

RETREATING — When a team returns to its defending zone because the opposing team gained possession of the

puck, it should remember to do two things:

- The forwards, especially the center, should keep their sticks on the ice when retreating on defense.
    - Easier to deflect an opponent's pass if the stick is already on the ice.
- When retreating on defense, the wingers should stay away from the boards, forcing the opposing wingers in that direction (farther from the goal).
    - Easier to deflect or intercept a pass.
    - A shot taken near the boards is usually more difficult because of the sharper angle to the goal.

CANUCKS 6, RANGERS 3

VANCOUVER . . . . .0 1 5—6
N.Y. RANGERS . . . . .0 0 3—3

First Period: None. **Penalties:** Hudson, Van (elbowing), :49; Molson, Van, minor-major (slashing, fighting), 10:06; Rollins, Van (roughing), 10:06; Benson, NY, minor-major-game misconduct (instigator, fighting), 10:06; Wesson, NY (high-sticking), 10:06; Mattson, NY (roughing), 10:06; Hudson, Van (roughing), 13:02; Wesson, NY (roughing), 13:02; Rollins, Van (holding), 17:20; Larson, NY (holding), 17:20; Nelson, NY (elbowing),19:42.

Second Period: 1, Vancouver, Broad 4 (Rollins, Anson), 8:10 (pp). **Penalties**: Melton, NY (hooking), 7:19; Cooper, Van, major (elbowing), 10:13.

Third Period: 2, Vancouver, Cooper 6, (Lancaster, Heyman), :26. 3, Vancouver, Burton 15 (Crandall), 2:48. 4, New York, Lipton 2 (Kotite), 3:27. 5, New York, Larson 9 (Mattson, Nen), 6:20 (sh). 6, New York, Melton 11 (Anders, Grant), 9:02. 7, Vancouver, Barber 3 (Burton), 9:31. 8, Vancouver, Cooper 7 (Larson, Lutz),12:20. 9, Vancouver, Burton 16 (Rollins),19:04 (en). **Penalty:** Kokov, NY (slashing),5:03. **Shots on Goal:** Vancouver 12-9-16—37. NewYork 17-7-14—38. **Goalies:** Vancouver, McKay 14-8 (38 shots - 35 saves). NewYork, Richardson 15-6 (36 - 31), Bolling (12:20 third, 6 - 6) **Attendance:** 15,663. **Referee:** Billy Chastman. **Linesmen:** Carl Lewiston, Paul Thomas.

GAME SUMMARY

A complete summary of the scoring and statistics of a hockey game. It appears in the sports page of the newspaper in addition to the narrative highlights of the game.

Includes the number of goals scored by each team in the three periods (and in the overtime period, if applicable).
- The visiting team is listed first.
- The home team is listed last.

Details regarding the goals in each period.
- The number of the goal scored during the game followed by the team that scored it.
    - If it was the sixth goal of the game, and it was scored by New York, it would read "6, New York."
- The player who scored the goal followed by his total of goals for the season.
- The player or players who were credited with an assist are listed in parentheses.
    - If the goal was scored without an assist, "unassisted" would appear next to goal scorer's name.
- The TIME OF THE GOAL, which is the time elapsed in the period when the goal was scored.
    - The time of the goal is not the time displayed on the game clock when the goal was scored. It is the time on the clock subtracted from 20:00, the length of a period.
    - If the clock shows 11:30 when a goal was scored, the time of the goal is 8:30 (20:00-11:30).
- A notation if the goal was scored when both teams did not have the same number of players or goalies on the ice.
    - (pp) Power Play — The scoring team had one or two more players on the ice than the opposing team.
    - (sh) Short-handed — The scoring team had

CANUCKS 6, RANGERS 3

VANCOUVER . . . . .0 1 5—6
N.Y. RANGERS . . . . .0 0 3—3

First Period: None. **Penalties:** Hudson, Van (elbowing), :49; Molson, Van, minor-major (slashing, fighting), 10:06; Rollins, Van (roughing), 10:06; Benson, NY, minor-major-game misconduct (instigator, fighting), 10:06; Wesson, NY (high-sticking), 10:06; Mattson, NY (roughing), 10:06; Hudson, Van (roughing),13:02; Wesson, NY (roughing), 13:02; Rollins, Van (holding), 17:20; Larson, NY (holding), 17:20; Nelson, NY (elbowing),19:42.

Second Period: 1, Vancouver, Broad 4 (Rollins, Anson), 8:10 (pp). **Penalties**: Melton, NY (hooking), 7:19; Cooper, Van, major (elbowing), 10:13.

Third Period: 2, Vancouver, Cooper 6, (Lancaster, Heyman), :26. 3, Vancouver, Burton 15 (Crandall), 2:48. 4, New York, Lipton 2 (Kotite), 3:27. 5, New York, Larson 9 (Mattson, Nen), 6:20 (sh). 6, New York, Melton 11 (Anders, Grant), 9:02. 7, Vancouver, Barber 3 (Burton), 9:31. 8, Vancouver, Cooper 7 (Larson, Lutz),12:20. 9, Vancouver, Burton 16 (Rollins),19:04 (en). **Penalty:** Kokov, NY (slashing),5:03.
Shots on Goal: Vancouver 12-9-16—37. NewYork 17-7-14—38. **Goalies:** Vancouver, McKay 14-8 (38 shots - 35 saves). NewYork, Richardson 15-6 (36 - 31), Bolling (12:20 third, 6 - 6) **Attendance:** 15,663. **Referee:** Billy Chastman. **Linesmen:** Carl Lewiston, Paul Thomas.

one or two fewer players on the ice than the opposing team.

- (en) Empty Net — The scoring team's goal took place when the opposing team had pulled its goalie.

Details regarding the violations resulting in penalties during each period.

- The guilty player and his team.
- The type of penalty and the violation.
    - If a type of penalty is not listed, the default is a minor penalty for a violation by a player that took place on the ice.
        1. A bench minor penalty would be noted because it results from either the violation not taking place on the ice or a non-player (a coach, for example) being guilty of the violation.
- The TIME OF THE PENALTY, which is the time elapsed in the period when the violation occurred. (See discussion above regarding TIME OF THE GOAL.)

The number of shots on goal each team attempted during each period and for the game.

The names of the goalies who played for each team.

- The goalies' season total of wins, losses and ties prints next to the WINNING GOALIE, the LOSING GOALIE or if it is a tie, the two TYING GOALIES of the game.
    - The winning goalie is on the ice when his team scores the GAME-WINNING GOAL.
        1. The goal scored that gave the team more goals than the opponents ended up scoring during the game.
        a. If the final score of a game was Florida 4, Edmonton 2, the third goal scored by Florida would be the game-winning goal.
        b. If the final score of a game was Florida 4, Edmonton 3, the fourth

CANUCKS 6, RANGERS 3

VANCOUVER . . . . .0 1 5—6
N.Y. RANGERS . . . . .0 0 3—3

First Period: None. **Penalties:** Hudson, Van (elbowing), :49; Molson, Van, minor-major (slashing, fighting), 10:06; Rollins, Van (roughing), 10:06; Benson, NY, minor-major-game misconduct (instigator, fighting), 10:06; Wesson, NY (high-sticking), 10:06; Mattson, NY (roughing), 10:06; Hudson, Van (roughing),13:02; Wesson, NY (roughing), 13:02; Rollins, Van (holding), 17:20; Larson, NY (holding), 17:20; Nelson, NY (elbowing),19:42.

Second Period: 1, Vancouver, Broad 4 (Rollins, Anson), 8:10 (pp). **Penalties**: Melton, NY (hooking), 7:19; Cooper, Van, major (elbowing), 10:13.

Third Period: 2, Vancouver, Cooper 6, (Lancaster, Heyman), :26. 3, Vancouver, Burton 15 (Crandall), 2:48. 4, New York, Lipton 2 (Kotite), 3:27. 5, New York, Larson 9 (Mattson, Nen), 6:20 (sh). 6, New York, Melton 11 (Anders, Grant), 9:02. 7, Vancouver, Barber 3 (Burton), 9:31. 8, Vancouver, Cooper 7 (Larson, Lutz),12:20. 9, Vancouver, Burton 16 (Rollins),19:04 (en). **Penalty:** Kokov, NY (slashing),5:03. **Shots on Goal:** Vancouver 12-9-16—37. NewYork 17-7-14—38. **Goalies:** Vancouver, McKay 14-8 (38 shots - 35 saves). NewYork, Richardson 15-6 (36 - 31), Bolling (12:20 third, 6 - 6) **Attendance:** 15,663. **Referee:** Billy Chastman. **Linesmen:** Carl Lewiston, Paul Thomas.

goal scored by Florida would be the game-winning goal.

- The losing goalie is on the ice when the opponents score the game-winning goal.
- The tying goalies are on the ice during the GAME-TYING GOAL.
    1. The last goal scored of a tie game.
        a. If Florida scored a goal in the third period making the score Florida 2, Edmonton 2 and that is how the game eventually ended, the second goal scored by Florida would be the game-tying goal.

- The number of shots on goal attempted while the goalie was on the ice and the number of saves he made.
    - The difference between these two figures is the goals he allowed while on the ice.
- If a substitute goalie enters the game, the time elapsed in the period and the period.

The attendance and the names of the officials.

As a result of his superb passing and scoring skills, Wayne Gretzky had four incredible 200-point seasons between the 1980-81 and 1986-87 seasons.

STATISTICS

PLUS/MINUS — Measures a player's offensive and defensive performance while he is on the ice.

- A plus is given to each player who is on the ice when his team scores a goal while the teams are at equal strength. Power-play and short-handed goals are ignored.
- A minus is given to each player who is on the ice when his team gives up a goal while the teams are at equal strength. Power-play and short-handed goals are ignored.
- At the end of the season a player definitely wants to have a net plus figure.

PLAYER'S POINTS — Total number of assists and goals scored by a player.

- If during the season, a player scored 20 goals and had 25 assists, he would have 45 points (20 + 25).

GOALS AGAINST AVERAGE — Average number of goals allowed in a sixty-minute game.

- Computed for each goalie by using the following ratio:

$$\frac{\text{Total goals}}{\text{Total minutes played}} \ \text{X} \ 60$$

- A goals against average under 2 is excellent.
- A goals against average over 4 is poor.

PENALTY MINUTES — Total number of minutes a player or team accumulates when serving a penalty for a violation.

- PENALTY MINUTES AVERAGE — Measures the length of time a team's players serve penalties each game.
    - Computed using the following ratio:

$$\frac{\text{Total penalty minutes}}{\text{Total games played}}$$

– Tends to highlight the most aggressive players and teams.

POWER PLAY PERCENTAGE — Measures the efficiency of a team scoring during its power play.
- Computed using the following ratio:

$$\frac{\text{Total power play goals scored}}{\text{Total power plays}}$$

- A power play percentage of 25% or more is excellent.
- A power play percentage of 15% or less is poor.

PENALTY-KILLING PERCENTAGE — Measures the efficiency of a team preventing a goal during an opposing team's power play.
- Computed using the following formula:

$$100\% \text{ minus the } \frac{\text{Total power play goals given up}}{\text{Total opposing team's power plays}}$$

- A penalty-killing percentage of 90% or more is excellent.
- A penalty-killing percentage of 75% or less is poor.

EASTERN CONFERENCE

ATLANTIC	W	L	T	PTS	GF	GA
NY Rangers	45	23	14	104	231	182
Philadelphia	45	24	13	103	274	217
NY Islanders	35	28	19	89	221	201
New Jersey	38	34	10	86	258	231
Washington	33	40	9	75	214	231
Tampa Bay	32	40	10	74	219	246
Florida	30	40	12	72	238	244

NORTHEAST	W	L	T	PTS	GF	GA
Boston	40	30	12	92	237	208
Pittsburgh	38	36	8	84	285	280
Ottawa	31	36	15	77	226	234
Montreal	31	36	15	77	249	276
Carolina	32	39	11	75	226	256
Buffalo	26	47	9	61	234	300

WESTERN CONFERENCE

CENTRAL	W	L	T	PTS	GF	GA
Chicago	48	26	8	104	280	203
Detroit	38	26	18	94	250	195
Phoenix	38	37	7	83	240	243
St. Louis	36	35	11	83	249	237
Dallas	34	35	13	81	223	210
Toronto	30	44	8	68	232	273

PACIFIC	W	L	T	PTS	GF	GA
Los Angeles	49	24	9	107	256	198
Anaheim	36	33	13	85	245	233
Edmonton	36	37	9	81	239	249
Vancouver	35	40	7	77	257	273
Calgary	32	41	9	73	214	239
Colorado	28	43	11	67	214	268
San Jose	27	47	8	62	211	278

LEAGUE STRUCTURE AND
TEAM STANDINGS

The NATIONAL HOCKEY LEAGUE (NHL) is the professional major league of hockey.

The STANDINGS show the position of each team within its division based on POINTS (discussed in detail below).

The NHL has two conferences, with two divisions in each conference.

EASTERN CONFERENCE   WESTERN CONFERENCE

Atlantic Division
Florida Panthers
New Jersey Devils
New York Islanders
New York Rangers
Philadelphia Flyers
Tampa Bay Lightning
Washington Capitals

Central Division
Chicago Blackhawks
Dallas Stars
Detroit Red Wings
Phoenix Coyotes
St. Louis Blues
Toronto Maple Leafs

Northeast Division
Boston Bruins
Buffalo Sabres
Carolina Hurricanes
Montreal Canadiens
Ottawa Senators
Pittsburgh Penguins

Pacific Division
Mighty Ducks of Anaheim
Calgary Flames
Colorado Avalanche
Edmonton Oilers
Los Angeles Kings
San Jose Sharks
Vancouver Canucks

Common abbreviations used in the standings:
- W (Wins) — The total wins by the team during the season.
- L (Losses) — The total losses by the team during the season.
- T (Ties) — The total ties by the team during the season.
- PTS (Points) — The total of points accumulated—2 points for each win and 1 point for each tie—by the team.

EASTERN CONFERENCE

ATLANTIC	W	L	T	PTS	GF	GA
NY Rangers	45	23	14	104	231	182
Philadelphia	45	24	13	103	274	217
NY Islanders	35	28	19	89	221	201
New Jersey	38	34	10	86	258	231
Washington	33	40	9	75	214	231
Tampa Bay	32	40	10	74	219	246
Florida	30	40	12	72	238	244

NORTHEAST	W	L	T	PTS	GF	GA
Boston	40	30	12	92	237	208
Pittsburgh	38	36	8	84	285	280
Ottawa	31	36	15	77	226	234
Montreal	31	36	15	77	249	276
Carolina	32	39	11	75	226	256
Buffalo	26	47	9	61	234	300

WESTERN CONFERENCE

CENTRAL	W	L	T	PTS	GF	GA
Chicago	48	26	8	104	280	203
Detroit	38	26	18	94	250	195
Phoenix	38	37	7	83	240	243
St. Louis	36	35	11	83	249	237
Dallas	34	35	13	81	223	210
Toronto	30	44	8	68	232	273

PACIFIC	W	L	T	PTS	GF	GA
Los Angeles	49	24	9	107	256	198
Anaheim	36	33	13	85	245	233
Edmonton	36	37	9	81	239	249
Vancouver	35	40	7	77	257	273
Calgary	32	41	9	73	214	239
Colorado	28	43	11	67	214	268
San Jose	27	47	8	62	211	278

- GAMES IN HAND — The additional number of remaining games a team has to play when compared to another team's remaining games.
    1. A factor in whether a team can increase its lead or overtake another team in the standings.
    2. A broadcaster might say, "The Blackhawks are 3 points behind the Blues but have two games in hand".
        a. If the Blackhawks won both games in hand, that would be worth 4 points and the Blackhawks would pass the Blues in the standings by 1 point (4 - 3).
- GF (Goals For) — The total number of goals scored by the team during the season.
- GA (Goals Against) — The total number of goals given up by the team during the season.

In the years before the 1993-1994 season, the names of the NHL's divisions and conferences were named after legends in hockey history. But starting with the 1993-1994 season, the names were changed to geographical references to simplify it for the fans.

- Wales Conference to Eastern Conference
    - Adams Division to Northeast Division
    - Patrick Division to Atlantic Division.
- Campbell Conference to Western Conference
    - Norris Division to Central Division.
    - Smythe Division to Pacific Division.

EASTERN CONFERENCE

ATLANTIC	W	L	T	PTS	GF	GA
X NY Rangers	45	23	14	104	231	182
X Philadelphia	45	24	13	103	274	217
X NY Islanders	35	28	19	89	221	201
X New Jersey	38	34	10	86	258	231
Washington	33	40	9	75	214	231
Tampa Bay	32	40	10	74	219	246
Florida	30	40	12	72	238	244

NORTHEAST	W	L	T	PTS	GF	GA
X Boston	40	30	12	92	237	208
X Pittsburgh	38	36	8	84	285	280
X Ottawa	31	36	15	77	226	234
X Montreal	31	36	15	77	249	276
Carolina	32	39	11	75	226	256
Buffalo	26	47	9	61	234	300

WESTERN CONFERENCE

CENTRAL	W	L	T	PTS	GF	GA
X Chicago	48	26	8	104	280	203
X Detroit	38	26	18	94	250	195
X Phoenix	38	37	7	83	240	243
X St. Louis	36	35	11	83	249	237
X Dallas	34	35	13	81	223	210
Toronto	30	44	8	68	232	273

PACIFIC	W	L	T	PTS	GF	GA
X Los Angeles	49	24	9	107	256	198
X Anaheim	36	33	13	85	245	233
X Edmonton	36	37	9	81	239	249
Vancouver	35	40	7	77	257	273
Calgary	32	41	9	73	214	239
Colorado	28	43	11	67	214	268
San Jose	27	47	8	62	211	278

X = team qualifies for the playoffs

PROFESSIONAL HOCKEY SEASON CYCLE

TRAINING CAMP — The four-week period during September when players get into shape, preparing for the regular season.

- Not only do teams practice among themselves, but they also play PRE-SEASON or EXHIBITION GAMES against other teams.
  - Often teams play exhibition games in cities without NHL teams in order to increase exposure for the league around North America.
- During training camp, coaches decide who will be on the team (sometimes called the ROSTER) for the beginning of the regular season.

REGULAR SEASON — The 82-game schedule each team plays from October to April.

- The primary objective of each team is to finish in first place, having the most points of all teams in its division, advancing to the playoffs.
- The secondary objective of each team is to have one of the top six number of points among the teams in its conference who did not finish in first place in their division. These teams also advance to the playoffs.
  - In the sample standings that are illustrated, the following teams would advance to the playoffs:
    1. Eastern Conference — NY Rangers and Boston for winning their divisions, and Philadelphia, NY Islanders, New Jersey, Pittsburgh, Ottawa and Montreal for being the next six teams with the most points in the conference.
    2. Western Conference — Chicago and Los Angeles for winning their divisions, and Detroit, Phoenix, St. Louis, Dallas, Anaheim and Edmonton for being the next six teams with the most points in the conference.

In the early years of hockey, teams only carried one goalie on their roster. For budget purposes, teams could not justify paying a salary to a player who might play only a few times during the year.

In Game 2 of the 1928 Stanley Cup finals between the New York Rangers and the Montreal Maroons, the Rangers goalie, Lorne Chabot, got hit in the eye with the puck and could not continue. None of the other Rangers could play goalie, so 44-year old coach, Lester Patrick told his team, "I'm going to play goal, fellows. Check as you've never checked before and help protect an old man."

The Rangers came out of the dressing room psyched up and played like animals. Patrick only allowed one goal and the Rangers won in overtime.

PLAYOFFS — Referred to as the STANLEY CUP playoffs because the winner is presented with the Stanley Cup trophy.

- Originally intended in 1893 by LORD STANLEY, the Governor General, to be presented to the top team in Canada.
  - Eventually awarded to the champion of the National Hockey League.
  - The names of the players and coaches on the winning team are engraved on the trophy.
  - The Cup sits in the HOCKEY HALL OF FAME just outside of Toronto.
    1. The treasured trophy is only removed for repairs, engraving or presentation.
- Four rounds of play in the two months following the regular season to determine the NHL champion.
  - In each conference, the two division winners are ranked 1 and 2 depending on who has the most points. The remaining six playoff teams in each conference are ranked 3 through 8, also based on number of points.
  - Round one — In each conference, the #1 ranked team plays the #8 team, #2 plays #7, #3 plays #6 and #4 plays #5. Teams play each other in a series of games that continues until one team wins four games.
    1. The maximum possible number of games in the first round series is seven, with one team winning four games and the other team winning three.
    2. Therefore, the length of the first round of the playoffs is said to be the BEST 4 OUT OF 7.
    3. The minimum number of games that could be played in a best 4 out of 7 series is four, with one team winning the first four games, ending the series.
  - Rounds two, three and the finals are also best 4 out of 7 series.
  - Regular season points in the standings determine which teams have the home ice

The third game of the 1975 Stanley Cup finals between the Philadelphia Flyers and the Buffalo Sabres was played in the worst conditions ever for a playoff hockey game. Buffalo's arena was not air conditioned and the temperature was extremely warm inside, melting patches of ice, resulting in a thick fog.

The game ended in overtime when the Sabres' Rene Robert smashed the puck past the Flyers' goalie, Bernie Parent, into the net. After the game, Parent told reporters, "I didn't have the *foggiest* notion where the puck was until it was too late."

advantage (a possible extra game played on its home ice) in each round of the playoffs.

1. In a best 4 out of 7 series, the first two games are played at the rink of the team that had more points. The third and fourth games are played at the other team's rink. If a fifth, sixth or seventh game is needed, the site alternates back and forth between the two teams' rinks.

- A tradition of sportsmanship always takes place at the end of a Stanley Cup series.
    - The teams line up near center ice and skate past each other, with all players shaking every opponent's hand in sportsmanship, no matter how intense and rough the series was.

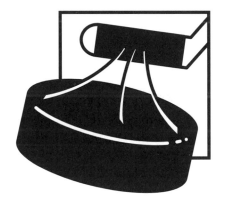

INDEX

HOCKEY QUIZ #1

1. In the regular season, if the teams are tied after three periods, *what happens*?

    a. The game ends in a tie.
    b. The first team to score in the 5-minute overtime period wins. If no team scores, then it is a tie.
    c. The teams continue playing and the game ends only when a touchdown is scored.
    d. The teams play another three periods.

2. A player at which of the following positions will *most likely score the most goals*?

    a. Forward.
    b. Defenseman.
    c. Goalie
    d. Netminder.

3. If a team has more players on the ice than the opponents because of penalties, *what is this called*?

    a. Hat trick.
    b. Shift.
    c. Power play.
    d. Breakaway.

4. A player is standing across the blue line in his attacking zone when his teammate, who has skated past the red line, passes the puck to him. *What happens next*?

    a. Play continues.
    b. Icing is called.
    c. Off-sides is called.
    d. A two-line pass is called.

5. Same as in question 4, except an opponent intercepts the pass in his defending zone and carries the puck over the blue line. *What happens next*?

    a. Play continues.
    b. Icing is called.
    c. Off-sides is called.
    d. A two-line pass is called.

6. A winger in his defending zone intercepts a pass and immediately passes the puck to his center who is already past the red line. *What happens next?*

    a. Play continues.
    b. Icing is called.
    c. Off-sides is called.
    d. A two-line pass is called.

7. Same as in question 6, except the pass to his center does not even touch him and eventually crosses the goal line before the opposing team's right defenseman touches the puck with his stick. *What happens next?*

    a. Play continues.
    b. Icing is called.
    c. Off-sides is called.
    d. A two-line pass is called.

8. A player begins serving a major penalty for charging. Four minutes later the opposing team scores a goal. *What happens next?*

    a. The player leaves the penalty box.
    b. A face-off takes place.
    c. The penalized player's team plays at full strength.
    d. All of the above.

9. A player is given a misconduct penalty for verbally abusing an official. *What happens next?*

    a. When the ten minutes of penalty time expires, the penalized player must wait until there is a face-off before entering the ice.
    b. A substitute may replace the penalized player immediately.
    c. If the goalkeeper is the guilty player, one of the players who was on the ice at that time serves the penalty.
    d. All of the above.

10. Which of the following penalties *does not cause the guilty player to be ejected from the game?*

    a. Game misconduct.
    b. Match.
    c. Third major of the game.
    d. Bench minor.

ANSWERS TO HOCKEY QUIZ #1

1. (b) A tie at the end of regulation play in the NHL results in sudden death overtime; the first team to score, wins. In a pre-season or regular season game, if neither team scores within the 5-minute overtime period, the game ends in a tie. (In playoff games, teams play as many 20-minute overtime periods until one team scores.)

2. (a) A forward normally scores more goals than a defenseman who focuses primarily on defense. A goalie (or sometimes called a netminder) has no scoring responsibility.

3. (c) A team is on the power play when it has more players on the ice than the opposition as a result of penalties. An easy way to remember it is that a team that outnumbers its opposition on the ice has more "power."

4. (c) Off-sides is the call because a player was already in his attacking zone when the puck entered the zone.

5. (a) Play continues. This is a delayed off-sides situation because while a player was in his attacking zone, the defending team immediately obtained possession of the puck after it crossed the blue line and passed the puck or carried it out of the zone.

6. (d) This is a two-line pass or also called an off-side pass. When a player passes the puck from its defending zone to a teammate who is beyond the red line at the center of the rink, a violation is whistled.

7. (b) If a pass originates from one side of the red line, crosses it and is first touched by an opposing player (other than the goalkeeper) after it crossed the goal line, icing is called. If an opponent could have touched the puck, the puck had passed through the goal crease, or the opponents were on a power play, icing is waved off and not called.

8. (b) The normal face-off after a goal is scored takes place. Unlike a minor penalty, if a player is in the penalty box for a major penalty and the opposing team scores a goal, the player may not leave the penalty box until the entire penalty time has expired.

9. (d) When a player is given a misconduct penalty, a substitute may enter the game while the guilty player goes to the penalty box. He may leave the box at the first stoppage of play after 10 minutes have expired. (The reason he cannot immediately leave the penalty box when the 10 minutes expire is that there would be too many men on the ice. Remember that the penalized player's team is not playing a man short as a result of the misconduct penalty.) Goalies do not serve misconduct penalties themselves.

10. (d) A bench minor penalty is issued for an infraction that is not severe enough to warrant suspending a player for the rest of the game (which is why it is called a minor penalty). An example includes a player on the bench arguing with an official.

HOCKEY QUIZ #2

Pretend you are an NHL team's coach in the following situations:

1. A penalty has been called on the opposing team while your team has possession of the puck in its defending zone. *What do you want your team to do next?*

   a. The player with the puck immediately shoot at your goal before the referee blows his whistle.
   b. Ice the puck to get it out of the zone.
   c. Your goalie immediately skates off the ice so that a forward can enter the game.
   d. Call a time out.

2. The opposing team is on a power play. One of your defensemen has the puck in his defending zone near the boards in the corner. *What do you want him to do next?*

   a. Pass the puck to your goalie.
   b. Center the puck.
   c. Poke check an opponent.
   d. Clear the puck out of the zone.

3. Your team has the puck in your defending zone. Your forwards and defensemen have been on the ice for almost 2 1/2 minutes and look tired. *What do you want them to do next?*

   a. Shoot the puck into the attacking zone so they can change on the fly.
   b. Carry the puck over the red line and then shoot the puck into the attacking zone so they can change on the fly.
   c. Pass the puck to a teammate between the red line and the attacking zone's blue line. He will then dump the puck into the zone so they can change on the fly.

d. Pass the puck to a teammate in the attacking zone so they can change on the fly.

4. Your team is losing by a goal with one minute and a half left in the game. *What would you instruct your team to do?*

   a. Call a time out during a breakaway.
   b. High stick an opponent who has the puck.
   c. Pull the goalie once the puck is in the neutral zone or your attacking zone.
   d. Shadow the opponent's top scoring forward.

5. Your left winger is trapped along the boards in your attacking zone by an opposing defensemen with the puck at his feet. He cannot get his stick free to make a pass. Your center is a couple of steps away without a defender near him. *What would you like to see your left winger do?*

   a. Reach down and knock the puck to your center with his hand.
   b. Kick the puck to your center.
   c. Cross-check the opposing player.
   d. Ice the puck.

6. Your defenseman is about to take a slap shot from the point. *What would you like to see one of your other forwards do?*

   a. Screen the goalie.
   b. Stand in the goal crease.
   c. Set up behind the goal.
   d. Set up near the red line.

7. An opposing player has taken control of the puck in his defending zone. *What should your team do to prepare for the counter attack?*

   a. Screen the goalie.
   b. Forecheck the puck carrier.
   c. Back-check the puck carrier.
   d. Dig the puck out of the corner.

8. Your left wing has the puck near the boards at the opponent's goal line. *What would you like him to do?*

   a. Screen the goalie.
   b. Center the puck.
   c. Clear the zone.
   d. Cross-check the opposing player.

9. An opposing player is on a breakaway. *What would you like to see your goalie do?*

   a. Move toward the shooter.
   b. Call a time out.
   c. Lift the goal posts out of the ice.
   d. Skate off the ice for another attacker.

10. Your player is on a breakaway. *Where would you like to see this left-handed player skate on the ice?*

    a. On the left side.
    b. On the right side.
    c. In the middle.
    d. No part of the ice gives him an advantage.

ANSWERS TO HOCKEY QUIZ #2

1. (c) When a penalty is called against the opposing team, you want your goalie to skate off the ice as quickly as possible so that an extra attacker can come into the game. There is no risk in leaving an empty net because the play ends once the opposing team gets control of the puck.

2. (d) By knocking the puck out of its defending zone, the opposing team on the power play must vacate the zone so that it will not be off-sides when the puck returns to that zone. Because icing is not called on a team defending against the power play, it is even better to knock the puck all the way to the other end of the ice—into your attacking zone. Remember the objective of penalty-killers is to use up time.

3. (b) A team in need of a substitution likes to dump the puck into its attacking zone. This way, the puck is furthest from its goal so it is less risky to substitute at that time. It is important to be across the red line before dumping the puck into the zone or icing will be called.

4. (c) Pulling the goalie is the strategy to use when losing late in the game. Your extra attacker that comes onto the ice gives the team a "power play advantage" and a better opportunity to score. Because this leaves an empty net defensively, the goalie is usually only pulled when the puck is in the neutral zone or your team's attacking zone.

5. (b) Kicking the puck to a teammate is allowed. A hand pass in your attacking zone is not permitted.

6. (a) Screening the goalie makes it difficult for the goalie to make the save. It is important that your attacker screening the goalie does not stand in the goal crease or interference may be called.

7. (b) The objective is to slow down the opponent's attack after an interception so that your players can set up defensively. Forechecking the puck carrier will slow his advancement. Your forechecker also might be able to take the puck away.

8. (b) When possible you want your players to center the puck where there is a high probability that the puck could be shot or deflected into the goal by another of your players.

9. (a) By coming out of the goal crease toward the breakaway player, your goalie cuts down the angle for the puck carrier to hit the puck into the goal. Also, the goalie covers up more of the goal visually as he approaches the puck carrier.

10. (c) When your player is on a breakaway it is better that he skates in the middle of the ice so that he has both corners of the goal as potential targets. On a breakaway, there is no advantage for the puck carrier to be left-handed or right-handed.

BIBLIOGRAPHY

Braine, Tim. *The Not-So-Great Moments in Sports.* New York: William Morrow, 1986.

Clark, Patrick. *Sports Firsts.* New York: Facts On File, 1981.

Considine, Tim. *The Language of Sport.* New York: Facts On File, 1982.

Copeland, Robert. *Webster's Sports Dictionary.* Springfield: G. & C. Merriam, 1976.

Eskenazi, Gerald. *A Thinking Man's Guide to Pro Hockey.* New York: E.P. Dutton, 1972.

Friedman, Arthur. *The World of Sports Statistics.* New York: Atheneum, 1978.

Hollander, Zander. *The Complete Encyclopedia of Hockey.* Detroit: Gale Research, 1993.

Hollander, Zander. *The Encyclopedia of Sports Talk.* New York: Corin Books, 1976.

Liss, Howard. *The Giant Book of Strange But True Sports Stories.* New York: Random House, 1976.

Malkovich, Andrew. *Sports Quotations.* Jefferson: McFarland & Co., 1984.

McFarlane, Brian. *Everything You've Always Wanted to Know about Hockey.* New York: Charles Scribner's Sons, 1971.

Nash, Bruce. *The Sports Hall of Shame.* New York: Pocket Books,1987.

National Hockey League. *Hockey Rules in Pictures.* New York: Perigee Books, 1992.

National Hockey League. *Official Rules 1996-97.* Chicago: Triumph Books, 1996.

Styer, Robert. *The Encyclopedia of Hockey.* New York: A.S. Barnes, 1970.

Sullivan, George. *Face-off: A Guide to Modern Hockey.* Princeton: D-Van Nostrand, 1968.

Sullivan, George. *This is Pro Hockey.* New York: Dodd Mead, 1976.

Walker, Henry. *Illustrated Hockey for Young People.* New York: Harvey House, 1976.

NCAA DIVISION I CHAMPIONS
—POST 1950

1950	Colorado College	1974	Minnesota
1951	Michigan	1975	Michigan Tech
1952	Michigan	1976	Minnesota
1953	Michigan	1977	Wisconsin
1954	Rensselaer	1978	Boston University
1955	Michigan	1979	Minnesota
1956	Michigan	1980	North Dakota
1957	Colorado College	1981	Wisconsin
1958	Denver	1982	North Dakota
1959	North Dakota	1983	Wisconsin
1960	Denver	1984	Bowling Green State
1961	Denver	1985	Rensselaer
1962	Michigan Tech	1986	Michigan State
1963	North Dakota	1987	North Dakota
1964	Michigan	1988	Lake Superior St.
1965	Michigan Tech	1989	Harvard
1966	Michigan State	1990	Wisconsin
1967	Cornell	1991	No. Michigan
1968	Denver	1992	Lake Superior St.
1969	Denver	1993	Maine
1970	Cornell	1994	Lake Superior St.
1971	Boston University	1995	Boston University
1972	Boston University	1996	Michigan
1973	Wisconsin	1997	North Dakota

NATIONAL HOCKEY LEAGUE
CHAMPIONS—POST 1950

1950–51	Toronto Maple Leafs	1974–75	Philadelphia Flyers
1951–52	Detroit Red Wings	1975–76	Montreal Canadiens
1952–53	Montreal Canadiens	1976–77	Montreal Canadiens
1953–54	Detroit Red Wings	1977–78	Montreal Canadiens
1954–55	Detroit Red Wings	1978–79	Montreal Canadiens
1955–56	Montreal Canadiens	1979–80	New York Islanders
1956–57	Montreal Canadiens	1980–81	New York Islanders
1957–58	Montreal Canadiens	1981–82	New York Islanders
1958–59	Montreal Canadiens	1982–83	New York Islanders
1959–60	Montreal Canadiens	1983–84	Edmonton Oilers
1960–61	Chicago Blackhawks	1984–85	Edmonton Oilers
1961–62	Toronto Maple Leafs	1985–86	Montreal Canadiens
1962–63	Toronto Maple Leafs	1986–87	Edmonton Oilers
1963–64	Toronto Maple Leafs	1987–88	Edmonton Oilers
1964–65	Montreal Canadiens	1988–89	Calgary Flames
1965–66	Montreal Canadiens	1989–90	Edmonton Oilers
1966–67	Toronto Maple Leafs	1990–91	Pittsburgh Penguins
1967–68	Montreal Canadiens	1991–92	Pittsburgh Penguins
1968–69	Montreal Canadiens	1992–93	Montreal Canadiens
1969–70	Boston Bruins	1993–94	NY Rangers
1970–71	Montreal Canadiens	1994–95	New Jersey Devils
1971–72	Boston Bruins	1995–96	Colorado Avalanche
1972–73	Montreal Canadiens	1996–97	Detroit Red Wings
1973–74	Philadelphia Flyers		

NATIONAL HOCKEY LEAGUE "MOST VALUABLE PLAYERS" —POST 1950 HART MEMORIAL TROPHY

Awarded annually in the NHL to the player "adjudged to be the most valuable to his team."

1950	Charlie Rayner, New York Rangers
1951	Milt Schmidt, Boston Bruins
1952	Gordie Howe, Detroit Red Wings
1953	Gordie Howe, Detroit Red Wings
1954	Al Rollins, Chicago Blackhawks
1955	Ted Kennedy, Toronto Maple Leafs
1956	Jean Beliveau, Montreal Canadiens
1957	Gordie Howe, Detroit Red Wings
1958	Gordie Howe, Detroit Red Wings
1959	Andy Bathgate, New York Rangers
1960	Gordie Howe, Detroit Red Wings
1961	Bernie Geoffrion, Montreal Canadiens
1962	Jacques Plante, Montreal Canadiens
1963	Gordie Howe, Detroit Red Wings
1964	Jean Beliveau, Montreal Canadiens
1965	Bobby Hull, Chicago Blackhawks
1966	Bobby Hull, Chicago Blackhawks
1967	Stan Mikita, Chicago Blackhawks
1968	Stan Mikita, Chicago Blackhawks
1969	Phil Esposito, Boston Bruins
1970	Bobby Orr, Boston Bruins
1971	Bobby Orr, Boston Bruins
1972	Bobby Orr, Boston Bruins
1973	Bobby Clarke, Philadelphia Flyers

1974	Phil Esposito, Boston Bruins
1975	Bobby Clarke, Philadelphia Flyers
1976	Bobby Clarke, Philadelphia Flyers
1977	Guy Lafleur, Montreal Canadiens
1978	Guy Lafleur, Montreal Canadiens
1979	Bryan Trottier, New York Islanders
1980	Wayne Gretzky, Edmonton Oilers
1981	Wayne Gretzky, Edmonton Oilers
1982	Wayne Gretzky, Edmonton Oilers
1983	Wayne Gretzky, Edmonton Oilers
1984	Wayne Gretzky, Edmonton Oilers
1985	Wayne Gretzky, Edmonton Oilers
1986	Wayne Gretzky, Edmonton Oilers
1987	Wayne Gretzky, Edmonton Oilers
1988	Mario Lemieux, Pittsburgh Penguins
1989	Wayne Gretzky, Los Angeles Kings
1990	Mark Messier, Edmonton Oilers
1991	Brett Hull, St. Louis Blues
1992	Mark Messier, New York Rangers
1993	Mario Lemieux, Pittsburgh Penguins
1994	Sergei Fedorov, Detroit Red Wings
1995	Eric Lindros, Philadelphia Flyers
1996	Mario Lemieux, Pittsburgh Penguins
1997	Dominik Hasek, Buffalo Sabres